JUST KEEP SWIMMING!

FISH BOOK FOR 4 YEAR OLDS

Children's Animal Books

Speedy Publishing LLC
40 E. Main St. #1156
Newark, DE 19711
www.speedypublishing.com

Copyright © 2017

All Rights reserved. No part of this book may be reproduced or used in any way or form or by any means whether electronic or mechanical, this means that you cannot record or photocopy any material ideas or tips that are provided in this book.

What makes a fish, a fish? Can they live outside of water? If they have to keep swimming, when do they sleep? Let's dive in to the world of fish!

Colorful coral reef with many fish

ALL THOSE COLD-BLOODED FISH

Clown Triggerfish.

Fish are animals that live in the water, in oceans, lakes, and rivers all over the Earth. Almost all fish have a few things in common:

- They have backbones (so they are "vertebrates").

- They breathe through gills, rather than having lungs. The gills draw oxygen out of the water, and then the fish expels the water. Fish can survive only a very short time if they are out of the water.

- They are cold-blooded. This means the temperature of their blood matches the temperature of the water they are in. Only a few species, like sharks, have a way of keeping warmer than the water around them.

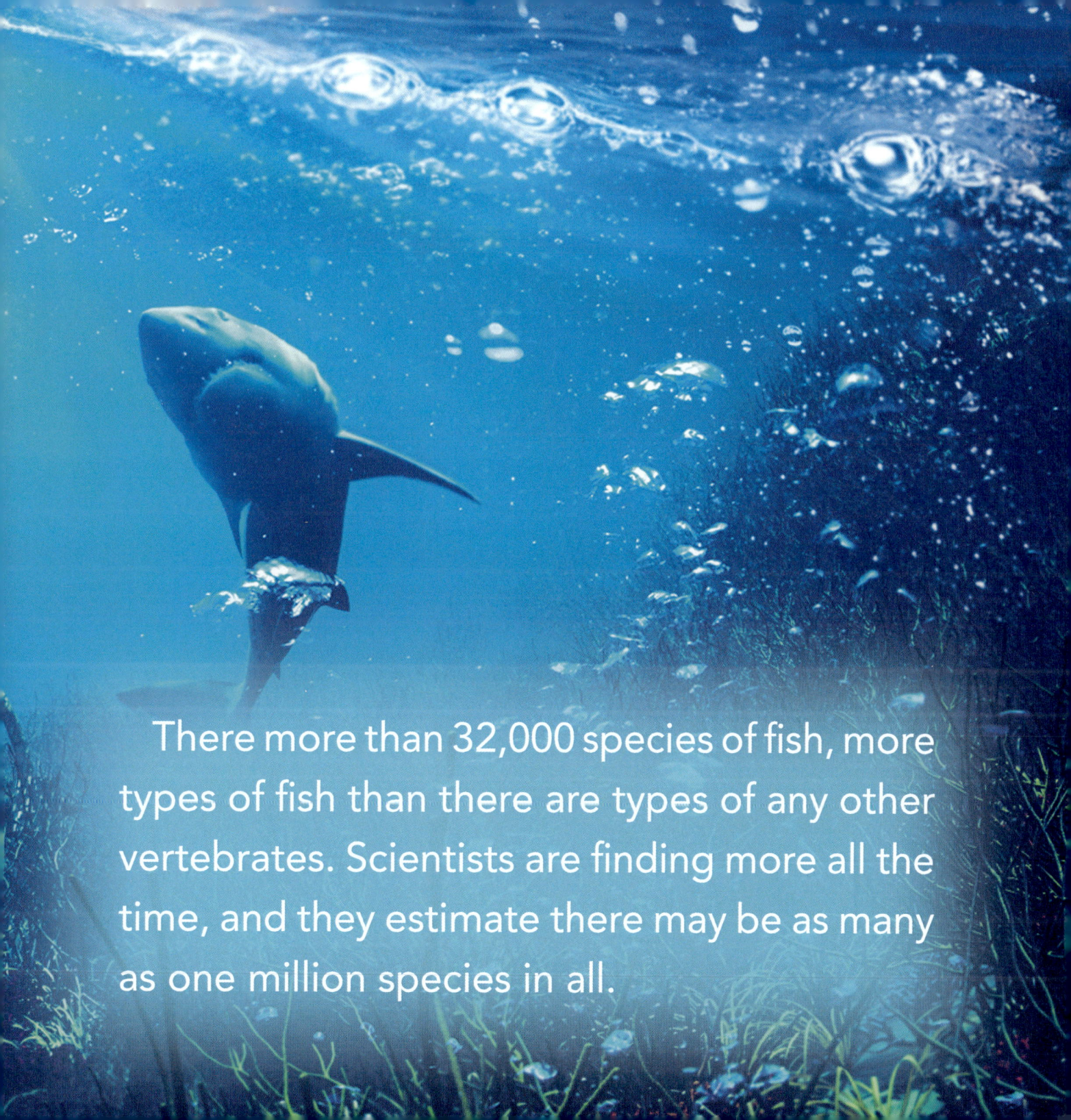

There more than 32,000 species of fish, more types of fish than there are types of any other vertebrates. Scientists are finding more all the time, and they estimate there may be as many as one million species in all.

Fish come in all sorts of shapes and colors, and some are even see-through! Most have scales, but some have rough skins. Most have fins that help them move through the water. Some can only live in fresh water, and others can only live in salt water; others, like **SALMON,** live most of the time in salt water in the oceans, and then swim up freshwater rivers and streams to lay their eggs in spawning grounds.

Sockeye Salmon jumping.

CLASSES OF FISH

Because there are so many species, scientists divide them into several classes. The main classes are:

- **JAWLESS FISH** – Jawless fish are like the *LAMPREY EEL*. It has a round mouth with lots of teeth, but no jaw so it can't really bite. It attaches itself to the side of another animal, like a suction cup, using the many rows of teeth in its mouth, and then gets nourishment from its host.

Lamprey Eel.

- **BONY FISH** - This is the largest class of fish. It includes little *GOLDFISH* in your fish tank at home, and the huge *TUNA* and *MARLIN* that can be as long as a small boat.

- **CARTILAGINOUS FISH** – The skeleton of a cartilaginous fish is made of cartilage, rather than bone. *SHARKS*, *SKATES*, and *RAYS* fall into this class.

Manta Ray.

Tropical Fish (Paracanthurus Hepatus)

NOT A FISH!

There are lots of creatures in the water that are not fish. Whales, seals, and sea lions are mammals: they started out as land animals, and over millions of years evolved for life in the ocean.

Breaching Humpback Whale.

Turtles and some other creatures are amphibians: they can live equally happily on the land or in the water.

A third group of non-fish water creatures are invertebrates, like *Jellyfish* and *Octopus*, that don't have backbones. There are also crustaceans, like *Lobsters* and bivalves like *Clams* and *Oysters*, that populate the sea without being fish.

Hawksbill Sea Turtle in Indian ocean.

Hammerhead Shark on the ocean floor

EATING AND BEING EATEN

Like all animals on the Earth, fish are part of the food chain. Many fish, especially the smallest ones, eat mainly plants like plankton. The larger fish eat both plants and smaller fish (when they can catch them!). Some of the largest fish, like the sharks, get most of their food by eating fish and other creatures like seals.

Plankton.

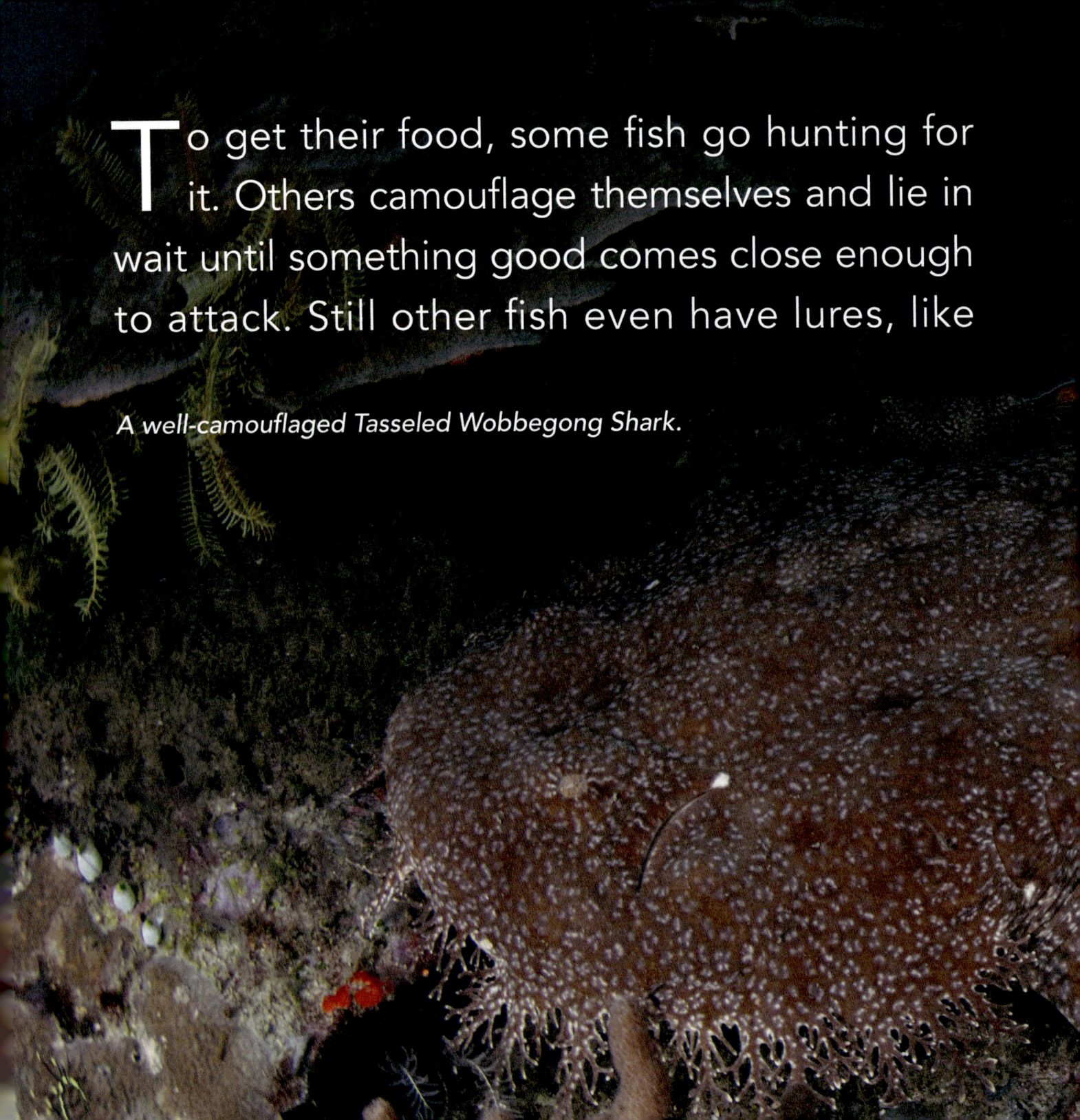

To get their food, some fish go hunting for it. Others camouflage themselves and lie in wait until something good comes close enough to attack. Still other fish even have lures, like

A well-camouflaged Tasseled Wobbegong Shark.

fishing lines with bright bobbles, dangling from their foreheads! When another fish comes close to investigate the shiny object, the fish with the lure gets its lunch delivered to it!

To avoid being eaten, some fish camouflage themselves or dig into the sand so they look like the bottom of the sea. Others hide in gaps between rocks or in coral reefs.

Broadhead Flathead Fish camouflaged on the sea bed.

Other fish travel in groups, or schools, hoping for safety in numbers. When a large fish attacks a school, the fish dodge away in different directions, and this can so confuse the attacker that he ends up with nothing in his mouth. A school of herring can have as many as three billion individual fish! People have reported seeing schools of mullet one hundred kilometers (60 miles) long in the Caspian Sea.

School of Fish.

Group of Tropical fish

SLICK FISH FACTS

Here are some great facts about fish of all kinds!

- Most fish lay eggs, but a few, like great white sharks, give birth to babies who are already able to swim and to hunt. Learn more in the Baby Professor book, *The Great White Shark.*

- A **LUNGFISH** has both gills and lungs. It uses the gills to get air when it is in water. When the water dries up in a lake, the lungfish hides under the mud and extends a breathing tube for air. The breathing tube brings air to its lungs. It can stay like that for years, until the lake has water again!

South American Lungfish.

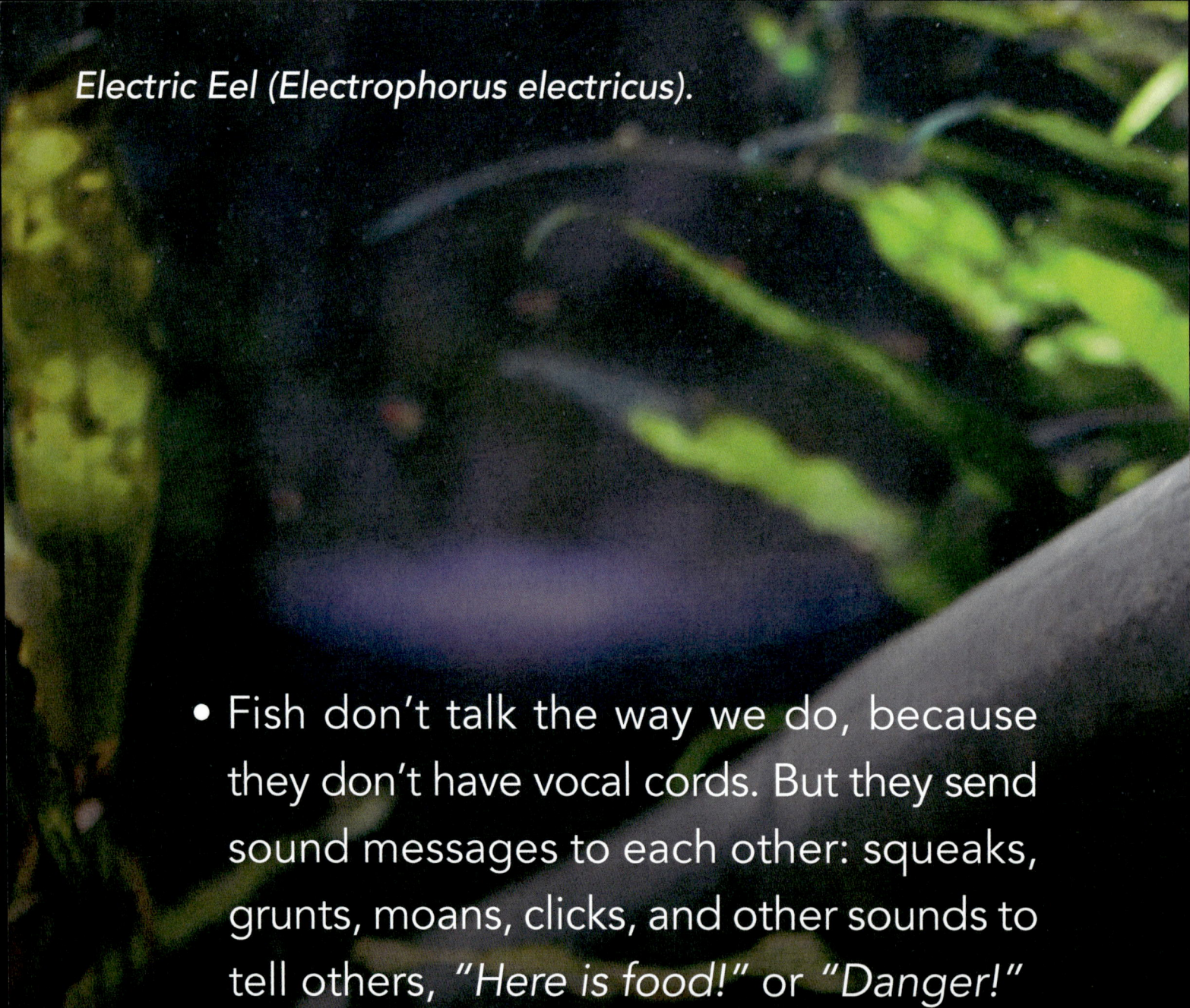

Electric Eel (Electrophorus electricus).

- Fish don't talk the way we do, because they don't have vocal cords. But they send sound messages to each other: squeaks, grunts, moans, clicks, and other sounds to tell others, *"Here is food!"* or *"Danger!"*

- An **ELECTRIC EEL** can generate enough voltage to shock and kill a horse.

- Fish don't really sleep the way we do. But they go through periods of lower activity while parts of their body go on swimming and avoiding running into rocks.

- The only fish with eyelids are **SHARKS.**

- Most fish have taste buds on their bodies. This helps them understand what is going on in the water around them.

- Once a **FLYING FISH** leaves the water, it can glide long distances, between 150 and 600 feet.

Flying Fish in the air.

- **SEAHORSES** are the only species of fish that swims in the upright position. However, they are not strong swimmers: if the weather is stormy and the water is rough, seahorses hang on to seaweed or something else to avoid dying of exhaustion.

Sea Horse of varying color.

- Most fish have *"swim bladders"* which they fill with enough air to help them stay at the water depth they prefer. They can let out or add air to change how deep they float. However, sharks and rays don't have swim bladders, so they have to keep swimming even when they are asleep. If they stopped swimming, they would sink to the sea bottom.

- When a **BATFISH** is in danger, it floats on its side on the surface of the water, trying to look like a dead leaf.

School of Batfish.

Four-eyed Fish (anableps anableps) floating on surface of water.

- There is a four-eyed fish called **ANABLEPS.** When it is near the surface, it has two of its eyes out of the water and two watching under the surface. This helps it look for things to eat and dodge creatures that want to eat it.

- **HAGFISH** defend themselves by making a coat of yucky slime all over themselves. A hagfish can fill a bucket with its slime in a minute. When the danger is over, the fish wrings itself out to get rid of the slime.

Goldfish

- **GOLDFISH** have teeth in their throats, not in their mouths. They gulp down their food and then use their **"pharyngeal teeth"** to crush it up.

Koi Carp

- When fish grow, their scales get bigger, You can see growth marks on the scales and tell how old the fish is, the same way you can tell how old a tree was by counting the rings in its trunk. A **KOI** that died in 1977 was estimated by its growth marks to have been born in 1751, so it was over 200 years old!

Sunfish

- A female **Sunfish** lays up to three hundred million eggs every year. Only a fraction of them hatch, and only a small proportion of the baby sunfish evade predators and grow up to adulthood.

Pygmy Goby

- The smallest adult fish, like the **Dwarf Pygmy Goby,** are no bigger than a grain of rice. At the other end of the scale, the whale shark can be sixty feet long and weigh more than 20 tons (even though it mainly eats plankton!).

- **The Peters Elephant Fish** may be the only fish species that plays with objects. In an aquarium, elephantfish will take a small object, like a ball of tinfoil, carry it to where the water flows into the tank, and release the ball so it can be pushed by the current. Then they will chase it and bring it back.

Peters' Elephantnose Fish.

- Most fish are darker on the top to match the ocean floor and lighter on the bottom to blend in with the light coming through the water from above. This makes them harder for predators to see.

Stingray city on Grand Cayman island.

- There is a fish you should never add to your fish tank: the **Malawi Eyebiter**. As its name suggests, this fish likes to snack on the eyeballs of its neighbor fish!

Malawi Eyebiter.

- **Cusk Eels** can live at high pressure, very deep in the ocean. One was brought up in a net from the very bottom of the Puerto Rico Trench, over twenty-seven thousand feet below the surface.

Giant Cusk Eel.

THE EARTH IS FULL OF LIFE!

Who lives in other parts of the earth? Find out in other Baby Professor books like *Vulnerable, Endangered, and Critically Endangered Animals: What are They?*, *Who Lives in the Tropical Rainforest?*, *Who Lives in the Barren Desert?* and *Insects and Arachnids*.

Banner fish.